TREASURES OF THE FATHERS OF THE CHURCH SERIES

Our paramount objective in this series is to introduce the believers to the trialogue of faith—the harmony among the Holy Bible, the Church Fathers, and the rites of the Coptic Orthodox Church. Through this symphony of discourse, the believer not only reads the Holy Scriptures, but understands it through the homilies, exegeses, and commentaries of the Church Fathers. This is a brief and simple companion to the Coptic Orthodox lectionary. We hope and pray that through this series, the Holy Bible, the Church Fathers, and the Church rites are not only introduced to each believer, but are experienced by the believer as a deep source of blessing, wisdom, and faith.

His Eminence Metropolitan Serapion
Editor-in-Chief

Father John Paul Abdelsayed
Father Ishak Boules Azmy
Father Moses Samaan
Series Editors

VOLUME I
Sunday Gospels of Tute-Amshir

VOLUME II
Sunday Gospels of the Great Lent

VOLUME III
The Holy Pascha

VOLUME IV
Sunday Gospels of the Holy Fifty Days

VOLUME V
Sunday Gospels of Baramhat-Nasie

VOLUME VI
Daily Readings for the Church Year

VOLUME VII
The Holy Theotokos

Ⲥⲩⲛ Ⲑⲉⲱ Ⲓⲥⲭⲩⲣⲟⲥ

On the Lord's Prayer

Saint Cyril of Alexandria

With a Preface by His Eminence Metropolitan Serapion

St. Paul Brotherhood Press
Coptic Orthodox Diocese of Los Angeles, Southern California, and Hawaii

ON THE LORD'S PRAYER

Saint Paul Brotherhood Press

Coptic Orthodox Diocese of Los Angeles, Southern California, and Hawaii
Saint Paul Brotherhood
38740 Avenida La Cresta
Murrieta, California 92562
www.SaintPaulBrotherhood.org

First Edition, July 2009
Second Edition, September 2017

ISBN 978-1-940661-96-4
LCCN 2013953851

Those who love riches, and whose mind is set on wealth and gain, gather by every means in their power the wished for object, and there is no labor they will not undertake. But their pursuit ends in no happy issue: "For what," as the Savior said, "profit is it to a man if he gains the whole world, and loses his own soul?" (Mt. 16:26). But those who love the Logos of salvation, and unroll the divine Scripture as a treasure, and carefully search out the things therein concealed, find the life-giving knowledge which leads them on to every virtuous pursuit, and makes them perfect in the knowledge of the doctrines of truth. Let us search therefore into the sense of the passage set before us. And our object is intelligently to see what the Savior commanded. For we must, He said, when we pray say, "Thy kingdom come." ... May our lot also be counted worthy of this great inheritance in Christ...

~Saint Cyril of Alexandria

His Holiness Pope Tawadros II
118th Pope of Alexandria and
Patriarch of the Great See of Saint Mark

His Eminence Metropolitan Scrapion
Metropolitan of Los Angeles,
Southern California, and Hawaii

Table of Contents

Preface

With great joy and enthusiasm, we present to you a collection of eight homilies delivered by St. Cyril of Alexandria, On the Lord's Prayer. These homilies are part of larger collection of sermons which St. Cyril seems to have preached extemporaneously, some on actual feast days. The original manuscripts of these homilies, preserved in Syriac, were discovered in Egypt, translated into English by Robert Payne Smith, and subsequently published by Oxford University in 1859. This was the first of St. Cyril's works to be translated into English.

Seven of the ten volumes in Migne's collection of the Cyrillian corpus contains the exegetical work of the great Alexandrian patriarch, most of which were written before his involvement in the Nestorian Controversy, before 428. This, along with his famous Commentary on the Gospel According to Saint John, are the only complete commentaries of the New Testament available. Unfortunately, only fragments of his commentaries on Matthew, Romans, 1 and 2 Corinthians and Hebrews are extant.

Within these homilies, St. Cyril seems to be citing Scripture from memory, that received text in the Alexandrian tradition as read in the church in the beginning of the fifth century. Generally, St Cyril follows the standard Septuagint Greek translation and the Theodotion version in others. Due to the complications of the Syriac rendering of the Greek, and other difficulties in the English translation of the Syriac, the Old Testament citations follow the English translation of the Septuagint found in the Apostles'

Bible, while the New Testament citations follow the New King James Version.

In the following homilies, the reader will be inspired by the intense, theological depth and spiritual vision of one of the greatest patriarchs the world has known. In this symphony of discourse, we witness how the harmony of the Holy Scriptures, the commentary of the Church Fathers, and the liturgical tradition blend to form a "trialogue" of faith that characterizes the fullness of Orthodox teaching.

We hope and pray that this series not only introduces each believer to the Holy Scriptures, the Church Fathers and the liturgical life of the Church, but also provides a deep source of blessing, wisdom and faith. Just as the Lord of Hosts promised to Baruch the prophet, "But I will give you life, as finding a treasure in every place, wherever you go" (Jeremiah 51:35), we experience that every place we search in the Scriptures with the fathers is a discovery of precious treasure for our souls–truly, the Pearl of great price, our Lord Jesus Christ.

Through the intercessions of the Holy Theotokos Saint Mary, which she makes for us; and the prayers of all His angels, St. Paul the Apostle, the rest of the apostles, the martyrs, St. Athanasius the Apostolic, St. Cyril the Pillar of Faith, and all the saints who have pleased Him since the beginning, we pray that this work will be a source of blessing for the glory of His Name and the spread of His Kingdom.

Glory be to the Holy Trinity, our God, unto the ages of all ages, Amen.

Metropolitan Serapion

I
Homily 70:

Lord Teach us to Pray
(Luke 11:1)

"Now it came to pass, as He was praying in a certain place, when He ceased, that one of His disciples said to Him, "Lord, teach us to pray, as John also taught his disciples."

So He said to them, "When you pray, say:

"Our Father in heaven, Hallowed be Your name. Your kingdom come. Your will be done on earth as it is in heaven. Give us day by day our daily bread. And forgive us our sins, for we also forgive everyone who is indebted to us. And do not lead us into temptation, but deliver us from the evil one." (Lk. 11:1-4)

O warm and fervent in spirit, now you also have come, and we beheld God's sacred court full of eager listeners. The purpose doubtless of your assembling is a pious one, and you have met together to be taught; and He Who is the Dispenser of the divine gifts, again satisfies you with those things of which you wish to be accounted worthy, and prepared a spiritual table, crying out saying, "Come eat of My Bread and drink the wine which I have mixed for you" (Prov. 9:5); and as the Psalmist says "Bread strengthens the heart of a man and the intellectual wine gladdens it" (Ps. 103:15).

Let us therefore draw near to the table now spread before us, even unto the signification of the gospel lessons: and let us attentively consider what advantage it brings us, and what it begets in us of these qualities which are necessary for the fitting honor of the saints.

Christ Did Not Pray Out of Personal Need

"Christ," it says, "was praying alone": and yet He is true God, and the Son of God over all; and Himself dispenses to the creation all those things by means of which it flourishes and is kept in being; and Himself is absolutely in need of nothing: for He is "full," as He said Himself (Is. 1:11, LXX).

"Of what then," someone asks, "is He in need, Who by right of nature possesses all that belongs to the Father? For He said plainly, 'All things that the Father has are Mine" (Jn. 16:15). But it is the property of the Father to be full of all good, and of such prerogatives as befit Deity; and this too belongs to the Son. And knowing this the saints say, 'And of His fullness we have all received' (Jn. 1:16). But if He gives as from His own godlike fullness, of what, can one say that He is in need, or what does He want to receive from the Father, as though He had it not already? And indeed, what does He pray for if He is full, and needs nothing that is the Father's!"

To this, we reply that He permits Himself, according to the manner of the dispensation in the flesh, to perform human actions whenever He wills, and as the season requires, without being liable to blame for so doing. For if He ate and drank, and is found partaking of sleep, what is there absurd, if also having humbled Himself to our measure, and fulfilled human righteousness, He not unfitly offered up prayer? And yet certainly He is in need of nothing, for "He is full," as we already said.

He Prays to Teach Us to Pray Silently and Alone

For what reason therefore, and in the performance of what necessary and profitable duty, did He pray? It was to teach us not to be slack in this matter, but rather to be constant in prayers, and very urgent; not standing in the middle of the streets; for this some of the Jews used to do, the scribes namely and Pharisees; nor making it an occasion of ostentation, but rather praying alone and silently, and by ourselves; and, so to speak, conversing alone with God alone, with pure and undistracted mind.

And this He clearly taught us in another place, saying of those who were wont to make a show of their prayers: "For they love to pray standing in the synagogues and on the corners of the streets, that they may be seen by men. Assuredly, I say to you, they have their reward. But you, when you pray, go into your room, and when you have shut your door, pray to your Father who is in the secret place; and your Father who sees in secret will reward you openly" (Mt. 6:5).

Unaccepted Prayer

For there are men who make a gain of the reputation of piety, and while earnestly attending to outward appearances, within are full of the love of vainglory. These often, when entering the church, first of all glance about in every direction, to observe the number of those standing there, and see whether they have many spectators. And as soon as the assembly pleases them, then raising their hand to their forehead, not once merely, but repeatedly they make there the sign of the precious Cross. And so spinning out a long prayer according to their own fancy, they babble in a loud tone, as though praying to the bystanders, rather than to God.

To such we say in the words of the Savior, "You have received your reward" (cf. Mt. 6:5) since you pray as hunting after the praises of men, and not as seeking anything of God. Your wish is fulfilled; you have been praised as being religious; you have gained vainglory: but you have traded in a fruitless labor; you have sown emptiness, and you shall reap nothing.

Do you want to see the end of your artifices? Hear what the blessed David says that "God has scattered the bones of those who please men" (Ps. 52:5). And by bones he here, of course, means not those of the body–for there are no instances of any men having suffered this– but rather the powers of the mind and heart, by means of which a man is able to effect good. The powers then of the soul are that earnestness which leads on strenuously to perseverance, spiritual strength, patience and endurance. These qualities God will scatter in such as please men.

In His Prayer, He Does Not Cease to Be Divine

In order, therefore, that we, withdrawing far from these disgraceful ways, and escaping from the snares to which they are exposed who seek to please men, may offer unto God prayer, holy, blameless and undefiled, Christ made Himself our example, by going apart from those who were with Him, and praying alone. For it was right that our Head and Teacher in every good and useful deed should be no other than He Who is first among all, and receives the prayers of all, and with God the Father bestows on those who ask Him whatever they require.

If, therefore, you see Him praying, as man, learn how to pray, do not withdraw from the belief and conviction that being by nature God Who fills all, He became like us and with us on earth as a man, and fulfilled human duties as the dispensation required: but that even so He was seated in heaven with the Father, dispensing of His own fullness all things to all, accepting the prayers of the dwellers upon earth, and of the spirits that are above, and crowned by them with praises. For He ceased not to be God by becoming like unto us, but continued even so to be whatsoever He had been.

For it became Him to be that which He had been, since He is unchangeable, and, as Scripture declares, not subject even to a "shadow of doubting" (cf. Jam. 1:17). But inasmuch as a long discourse is required for what remains, holding it in for the present, as it were, with a bridle, lest it should become tedious to the hearers, we will hereafter with God's help explain it to you, when next Christ the Savior of us all assembles us here: by Whom and with Whom, to God the Father be praise and dominion with the Holy Spirit forever and ever, Amen.

II
Homily 71:

Our Father Who Art in Heaven
(Luke 11:1)

Our Lord Jesus Christ counted the unsatisfied desire of learning as worthy of all praise, thus saying, "Blessed are those who hunger and thirst for righteousness, for they shall be filled." (Mt. 5:6). For it is right constantly to hunger and thirst after those things, by means of which a man becomes a warm lover of saintly glories, and earnest in every good work. And to all who are thus minded, Christ reveals the way by which they can accomplish their desire. But serviceable is it above all things besides for the religious unto salvation, that they know how to pray, and offer not supplications displeasing to Almighty God. For as the wise Paul wrote to us, "For we do not know what we should pray for as we ought" (Rom. 8:26). Let us therefore draw near unto Christ, the Giver of wisdom, and say, "Lord, teach us to pray" (Lk. 11:1). Let us be like the holy apostles, who above all other things asked of Him this profitable and saving lesson.

Now at our last meeting we heard the gospel read, which says of Christ, the Savior of us all, that "It came to pass, that as He was in a certain place praying by Himself." And we addressed you, explaining as well as we could the dispensation, by reason of which Christ prayed: and when we had carried our argument to this point, we reserved the rest for some fitting occasion. This has now arrived, and is present. Let us then proceed to what follows; for the Savior said, "When you pray, say, 'Our Father.'" And another of the holy evangelists adds, "Who art in heaven" (cf. Mt. 6:9).[1]

---

[1] St. Cyril notices below that the sentence, "Who art in heaven," was not found in St. Luke's Gospel. Its insertion therefore here is because the

O boundless liberality! O incomparable gentleness, and that befits Him alone! He bestows upon us His own glory: He raises slaves to the dignity of freedom. He crowns man's estate with such honor as surpasses the power of nature: He brings that to pass which was spoken of old by the voice of the Psalmist: "I said, you are gods; and all of you children of the Most High" (Ps. 82:6). For behold! He rescues us from the measure of slavery, bestowing upon us by His grace that which by nature we possessed not: and permits us to call God "Father," as being admitted to the rank of sons.

Of Him have we received this, together with all our other privileges: and the wise John the Evangelist witnesses to this, thus writing of Him, "He came to His own, and His own did not receive Him. But as many as received Him, to them He gave the right to become children of God, to those who believe in His name: who were born, not of blood, nor of the will of the flesh, nor of the will of man, but of God" (Jn. 1:11-13).

For we have been fashioned unto the sonship by that birth which is spiritually wrought in us, "not of corruptible seed but incorruptible, through the word of God which lives and abides forever" (1 Pet. 1:23), as Scripture says. "Of His own will He brought us forth by the word of truth, that we might be a kind of firstfruits of His creatures," for so one of the holy apostle declares (Jam. 1:18). And Christ Himself, in a certain place, clearly explained the manner of this birth by declaring; "Most assuredly, I say to you, unless one is

---

fuller form given by St. Matthew was that best known having been adopted in the liturgical tradition: or possibly from St. Cyril's habit of quoting St. Matthew's Gospel in preference to St. Luke's.

born of water and the Spirit, he cannot enter the kingdom of God" (Jn. 3:5).

Or rather–for to you it is right to speak even of those things that are mysterious–He Himself became both the Way and the Door (cf. Jn. 14:6, 10:9) and the cause of a grace being bestowed upon us thus glorious and worthy of our gaining by having taken upon Him our likeness. For although in that He is perceived to be, and is God, He is free, yet He took the form of a slave, that He might bestow upon us those things which are His, and enrich the slave with His own excellencies (cf. Phil. 2:7). For He alone is by nature free, because He alone is Son of the Father, even of Him Who is supreme above all, and rules over all, and Who is by nature and verily free. For whatever has been brought into existence bows the neck of slavery to Him Who created it.

For the Psalmist chants unto Him, saying, that "All things are Your slaves" (Ps. 118:91); but inasmuch as in the dispensation He transferred to Himself what was ours, He has given us what was His.[2] And the most wise Paul, the minister of His mysteries, is our proof, thus writing, "that though He was rich, yet for your sakes He became poor, that you through His poverty might become rich" (2 Cor. 8:9). For our things, by which is meant the condition of human nature, is poverty to God the Logos: while it is wealth to human nature to receive what things are His. And

---

[2] This phrase again resembles the refrain of the Friday Theotokia, "He took what is ours and gave us what is His. We praise and glorify Him we highly exalt Him." A similar phrase is also fond in St. Cyril's That Christ is One: "He took what was ours to be His very own so that we might have all that was His."

of these one is the dignity of freedom–a gift peculiarly befitting those who have been called to sonship.

And this, as I mentioned, is also His gift: for He said unto us, "Do not call anyone on earth your father; for One is your Father, He who is in heaven" (Mt. 23:9). And again, He Himself too, from His infinite love to mankind, is not ashamed to call us brethren, thus saying; "I will preach Your name to My brethren" (Ps. 21:23). For because He became like unto us, we thereby have gained brotherhood[3] with Him.

He commands us, therefore, to take boldness and say in our prayers, "Our Father." We children of earth and slaves, and subject by the law of nature to Him Who created us, call Him Who is in heaven "Father."

And most fittingly He makes those who pray understand this also: that if we call God "Father," and have been counted worthy of so distinguished an honor, must we not necessarily lead holy and thoroughly blameless lives, and so behave as is pleasing to our Father, and neither think nor say anything unworthy or unfit for the freedom that has been bestowed upon us? And so one of the holy apostles spoke: "And if you call on the Father, who without partiality judges according to each one's work, conduct yourselves throughout the time of your stay here in fear;" (1 Pet. 1:17). For it is a most serious thing to grieve and provoke a father, by turning aside unto those things which are not right.

[3] Of course, St. Cyril uses this term "brotherhood" in such a way to indicate Our Lord Christ as the One and Only natural Son of God; while believers become the adopted children of God through the Mystery of Holy Baptism.

How do earthly fathers act, or what is their feeling towards their sons? When they see them willing to conform themselves to their wishes, and choosing that course of conduct which is pleasing to them, they love and honor them; they open to them their house; they multiply their presents of whatever they wish, and acknowledge them as their heirs. But if they are disobedient and unyielding, having no respect for the laws of nature, and indifferent to that affection which is implanted in us, they drive them from their house and deem them unworthy of any honor, indulgence, or love. They even refuse to acknowledge them as sons, and do not write them as their heirs.

Ascend now, I pray, from things as they are with us to those that transcend us. You call God "Father"; honor Him with ready obedience; yield submission as that which is His due; live so as He pleases; show not yourself harsh or proud, but, on the contrary, yielding and submissive, and ready without delay to follow His directions, so that He may honor you in return and appoint you fellow-heir with Him Who is the Son by nature. For if "He who did not spare His own Son, but delivered Him up for us all, how shall He not with Him also freely give us all things," according to the expression of the blessed Paul (Rom. 8:32)? But if you have no regard for yourself, and therefore do not heed the bountiful gift that is bestowed, you are proved to be bold, and, so to speak, without salt, loving pleasure more than you love the Father.

Fear, therefore, lest God say of you the same which was spoken concerning the Israelites by the word of Isaiah: "Hear, O heavens; and give ear, O earth, for the Lord has spoken: I have begotten and brought up children, but they have rejected Me" (Is. 1:2). Heavy in every way, my beloved, is the guilt of those who rebel; and most wicked the crime of rejecting (God). Very wisely therefore, as I said, does the Savior of all grant us to call God "Father," that we, well knowing that we are sons of God, may behave in a manner worthy of Him Who has thus honored us; for so He will receive the supplications which we offer in Christ: by Whom and with Whom to God the Father be praise and dominion, with the Holy Spirit, forever and ever, Amen.

III
Homily 72:

Hallowed be Thy Name
(Luke 11:2)

All who desire the sacred words of God, the prophet Isaiah commands, saying, "You who thirst come to the waters" (Is. 55:1). For who may draw from the life-giving Fountain? And Who is this Fountain? Plainly, it is Christ and His doctrines. For He has somewhere said unto us, "If anyone thirsts, let him come to Me and drink" (Jn. 7:37). Let us then again come as to a fountain; let us fill our souls; let us satiate ourselves from the torrent of pleasure. For the blessed David somewhere in a psalm thus speaks of Him unto God the Father: "They shall be satisfied with the fatness of Your house: and You will make them drink of the torrent of Your pleasure. For with You is the fountain of life" (Ps. 35:9). For the river of pleasure is richly poured forth for us, and the fountain of life, even that which is in Christ, Who also by one of the prophets has thus spoken concerning us: "Behold, I bend down unto them as a river of peace, and as a torrent flooding them with the glory of the Gentiles" (Is. 66:12).

For observe how Christ waters us with rich streams of spiritual blessings. For what will He teach us next? When you pray, He says, say, "Our Father...Hallowed be Thy Name." Now behold! Already we have discoursed unto you not without profit, when explaining in what manner it is right for us to say, "Our Father." And you, I think, remember my words, in that you are, as I said, eager after learning. In order, therefore, that we may not say the same things; for that were tedious to attentive listeners, who store up in the treasure-house of their heart whatever they have already understood, and wish constantly to advance unto something further, let us proceed to that which follows, namely, "Hallowed be Thy Name," and let us consider in what way this also must be understood.

Do we then pray that additional holiness may accrue unto the All-Holy God? And how would not this be absolutely absurd? For if indeed there is anything wanting to God over all, in order to his being perfect, and in need of nothing, He may need additional holiness: but if He is full, as He says (Is. 1:11), and in every respect perfect in and by Himself, and the Giver of holiness to the creation out of His own fulness; what addition can He receive? For all things are His, and He has reached the highest perfection in every good: for this is also an attribute of His by nature. And besides it is a foolish and ridiculous thing for those who pray to imagine that they offer their supplications not on their own behalf but on His.

What therefore is the meaning of "Hallowed be Thy Name?" We say then, that men do not supplicate for any addition of holiness to accrue unto God over all: for who is greater than He, and able to give Him any increase? "Now beyond all contradiction the lesser is blessed by the better" (Heb. 7:7). But they supplicate rather that this may be granted unto them and all mankind.

To Hallow God is to Live a Holy Life

For when it is our settled conviction and belief, that He Who by nature is God over all, is Holy of the Holies, then we confess His glory and supreme majesty; then we receive His fear into our mind, and lead upright and blameless lives, that by thus becoming ourselves holy, we may be able to be near unto the holy God. For it is written, "Become holy: for

I am holy" (Lev. 11:44). And He once also said to the hierophant Moses, "I will be hallowed in those who draw near to Me" (Lev. 10:3). The prayer, therefore, is "May Thy Name be kept holy in us, in our minds and wills." For this is the signification of the word, "hallowed."

For just as one who suffers under a disease in his bodily sight, and is able to see but little, and with difficulty; and prays, saying, "O Lord of all, grant that the light of the sun's radiance may illuminate me also," does not, we affirm, make his supplications on the sun's behalf, but, on the contrary, upon his own. So also if a man say, "Our Father...Hallowed be Thy Name," he is not requesting any addition be made to God's holiness, but rather asks that he may himself possess such a mind and faith, as to feel that His Name is honorable and holy. The act, therefore, is the source of life, and the cause of every blessing; for to be thus affected towards God, how must it not be a thing worthy of the highest estimation, and useful for the salvation of the soul?

To Hallow God is to Pray for the Whole World

But, do not imagine that when those who depend upon His love are earnest in their supplications towards God, that they ask these things from Him for themselves alone. But know, rather, that their purpose is to intercede for all the dwellers upon earth: for those who already have believed and for those who have not as yet received the faith nor acknowledged the truth. For those who have already believed ask that their faith may be established and that they may be able to practice the glories of the more excellent life. While, those who are not yet believers ask that they may be called and their eyes opened, even in this following the footsteps of Christ, Who according to the words of John is the "Advocate with the Father...for our sins, and not for ours only, but also for the whole world" (1 Jn. 2:1). Therefore He Who is the Intercessor for the saints, and for the whole world, wills that His disciples be like Himself.

To Hallow God is to Regard Him as Holy and to Fear Him

When therefore men say to the Father, "Hallowed be Thy Name," remember, that among those who have not yet gained the light of truth, nor received the faith, the Name of God is despised. It does not yet seem to them to be holy, honorable, and adorable. But no sooner has the light of truth risen upon them, and they have with effort awoke as from some night and darkness, then learning Who and how great He is, they acknowledge Him as Holy of the Holies, and have correspondent sentiments and belief.

But that the phrase, that God is hallowed by us, is a confession of our regarding Him as Holy of Holies, and does not bestow on Him any additional holiness, you may understand the following.

One of the holy prophets said, "Hallow the Lord, and He shall be Your fear: and if you trust in Him, He shall be holiness unto you" (Is. 8:13). Do we then make God holy? Is it the act of human nature to bestow anything at all on God? Does the thing made benefit the Maker? Does any man imagine that He, Who of His fulness richly distributes unto the creature His gifts, will Himself receive anything at all of us, whose place it is to listen to the words of the blessed Paul, "And what do you have that you did not receive?" (1 Cor. 4:7). When, therefore, the prophet said,

"Hallow the Lord, and He shall be your fear, and holiness unto you," we affirm that what He teaches is, "Believe that

He is holy, for then you will fear Him; and so He will thus be to you the means of holiness."

To Hallow Him is to Confess His Divinity in His Incarnation

And it is written again of Christ the Savior of us all; "Hallow Him, Who despised Himself" (Is. 49:7). For He did despise Himself, by deeming His life of no account, and laying it down for our sakes. But let Him be hallowed, it says, by you: that is, let Him be acknowledged as holy. For such He is by nature, as being very God, and the Son of God. For to be essentially holy suits not anyone whatsoever of those things, which from nonexistence have been brought into being: but only that supreme nature which transcends all. By believing therefore that He is by nature holy–for this is the meaning of our hallowing Him–we further acknowledge Him to be very God.

For ourselves, therefore, and not for God let us pray, saying, "Hallowed be Thy Name." For if we are thus disposed, and with a free mind offer up prayers such as this, God the Father will accept us, and Christ with Him will bless us: by Whom and with Whom to God the Father be praise and dominion, with the Holy Spirit, forever and ever, Amen.

IV
Homily 73:

Thy Kingdom Come
(Luke 11:2)

Those who love riches, and whose mind is set on wealth and gain, gather by every means in their power the wished for object, and there is no labor they will not undertake. But their pursuit ends in no happy issue: "For what," as the Savior said, "profit is it to a man if he gains the whole world, and loses his own soul?" (Mt. 16:26). But those who love the Logos of salvation, and unroll the divine Scripture as a treasure, and carefully search out the things therein concealed, find the life-giving knowledge which leads them on to every virtuous pursuit, and makes them perfect in the knowledge of the doctrines of truth. Let us search therefore into the sense of the passage set before us. And our object is intelligently to see what the Savior commanded. For we must, He said, when we pray say, "Thy kingdom come."

God is the Eternal King with an Eternal Kingdom

Nevertheless, He reigns over all with God the Father: nor can any addition be made to His kingly glory, either as accruing to Him from without, or as given Him by another. Nor did it gather by the course of time, but, so to speak, sprang up with Him without a beginning. For He always was and is that which He was. Altogether therefore, and in every way it follows upon His being God by nature and verily, that He must be Omnipotent, and that this glorious attribute is, so to speak, His without a beginning, and without end.

For one also of the holy prophets said unto Him, "The Lord reigns forever and ever" (Ex. 15:18). And the divine Psalmist also says, "Your kingdom is a kingdom of all ages" (Ps. 144:13). And again, "God is our king before the ages"

(Ps. 73:12). Since, therefore, God ever reigns, and is Omnipotent, with what view do those who call God Father offer up to Him their supplications, and say, "Thy kingdom come?"

He Will Come to Judge the Living and the Dead

They seem, therefore, to desire to behold Christ the Savior of all rising again upon the world. For He will come, He will come and descend as Judge, no longer in low estate like unto us, nor in the simplicity of human nature; but in glory such as befitting of God, for He dwells in unapproachable light (cf. 1 Tim. 6:16), and with the angels as His guards. For so He somewhere Himself said that "the Son of Man comes in His glory, and all the holy angels with Him" (Mt. 25:31). And I think, therefore, that I should also add that at the consummation of this world He will descend from heaven, but no longer to instruct those on earth, as He did of old, nor again to show them the way of salvation–[for] the season for this has passed away–but to judge the world.

And the wise Paul also bears witness to what I say, declaring that, "we must all appear before the judgment seat of Christ, that each one may receive the things done in the body, according to what he has done, whether good or bad" (2 Cor. 5:10). Terrible, therefore, is that judgment seat; without respect of persons is the Judge; it is a time of pleading, or rather of trial, and of retribution. The fire is prepared for the wicked, and enduring punishment, and eternal torments.

The Careless Will be Punished

And how can men pray to behold that time? Observe, I pray again, the Savior's skillfulness, and His admirable management in every particular. For He commanded them to ask in prayer that this fearful time may come, to make them know that they must live, not carelessly, nor dissolutely, nor moreover as beguiled into laxity and the love of pleasure; but, on the contrary, as becomes saints, and according to God's will: that so that this fearful time may prove the bestower upon them of crowns, and not of fire and condemnation. For it was not at all proper for the wicked and impure–who lead base and lascivious lives, guilty of every vice–in their prayers to say, "Thy kingdom come."

Rather let them know that in so saying they, as it were, charge God with blame, because the time of their punishment does not quickly arise and manifest itself. Of them one of the holy prophets said, "Woe unto those that desire the day of the Lord! What will the day of the Lord be unto you? For it is darkness, and not light; and that thick darkness in which is no brightness" (Amos 5:18).

The Saints are Good Stewards Who are Ready

The saints, therefore, ask that the time of the Savior's perfect reign may come, because they have labored dutifully, and have a pure conscience, and look for the requital of what they have already wrought. For just as those who are expecting a festival and merriment about speedily to come, and shortly to appear, thirst for its arrival, so also do they. For they trust that they shall stand glorious in the presence of the Judge, and hear Him say: "Come, you blessed of My

Father, inherit the kingdom prepared for you from the foundation of the world" (Mt. 25:34). They were wise and zealous stewards when their Lord set them over His household to give them their food in its season.

Well and wisely did they distribute to their fellow servants those things by the receiving of which they had themselves before been made rich; for they remembered Him Who said, "Freely you have received, freely give" (Mt. 10:8). When they received of Him the talent, they did not bury it in the earth. They were not like that slothful, lazy, and careless servant, who drew near, saying: "Lord, I knew you to be a hard man, reaping where you have not sown, and gathering where you have not scattered seed. And I was afraid, and went and hid your talent in the ground. Look, there you have what is yours" (Mt. 25:24-25).

They, on the contrary, traded; and so they brought it greatly multiplied, saying, "Master, your mina has earned ten minas" (Lk. 19:16) and were admitted to yet further honors. They "have put on the whole armor of God," the breastplate of righteousness, the helmet of salvation, and have taken the sword of the Spirit (cf. Eph. 6:11, 13-16). It did not escape them that they had a war, not "against flesh and blood, but against principalities, against powers, against the rulers of the darkness of this age, against spiritual hosts of wickedness in the heavenly places" (Eph. 6:12).

For many wove for themselves crowns of martyrdom, and by enduring conflicts, even unto life and blood, were made "a spectacle to the world, both to angels and to men" (1 Cor. 4:9) and were accounted worthy of all admiration. There were others who endured labors and persecutions, eagerly contending for His glory. "Savage wolves" sprang in upon Christ's flocks, "not sparing the flock," as the divine Paul declares (Acts 20:29). "Deceitful workers," "false apostles," (2 Cor. 11:13) vomiting forth the gall of the malice of the devil and "speaking perverse things" (Acts 20:30), such as lead ignorant souls to destruction, and "wound their weak conscience" (1 Cor. 8:12). These, by flattering the powers of this world, brought persecutions and distresses upon the champions of the truth. But, they made no great account of what they suffered, for they looked unto the hope which they had in Christ. For it was known to them that by suffering for Him they would reign with Him (cf. 2 Tim. 2:12). They knew that at the time of the resurrection, He will transform the body of their humiliation into the likeness of His glorious body (cf. Phil. 3:21). They fully believed what He said about the consummation of the world, that when He shall appear to them again from heaven, they "will shine forth as the sun in the kingdom of their Father" (Mt. 13:43).

Justly, therefore, in their prayers they say, "Your kingdom come." For they feel confident that they shall receive a recompense for their bravery, and attain to the consummation of the hope set before them.

May our lot also be counted worthy of this great inheritance in Christ; by Whom and with Whom to God the Father be praise and dominion, with the Holy Spirit, forever and ever. Amen.

V
Homily 74:

Thy Will be Done, on Earth as it is in Heaven
(Luke 11:2)

The prophet David made his supplications to Christ the Savior of all, saying, "Lead me in Your truth and teach me that You are the God of my Salvation" (Ps. 24:5). For all those who are in Christ by faith are taught by God; and among these are we.

Of Him, therefore, let us ask the explanation of His words. For whoever would understand correctly and without error what He wishes to teach, are in need of divine light. But He is the Giver of all wisdom, and sheds His light upon the mind and heart of those that ask Him. For again the Psalmist said, "Unveil my eyes, and I shall behold the wonders out of Your law" (Ps. 118:18). Let us, therefore, examine this part also of the prayer: for it will profit us in no slight degree to the salvation of the soul. Why then did He command the saints to say unto God the Father in heaven, "Thy will be done; on earth as it is in heaven"?

The Will of God is to Serve Him Spiritually and Worship Him

Worthy of the saints and full of all praise is this petition also. Thus, for them to ask that the goodwill of God may prevail on earth, what else is it but to ask that all mankind may lead praiseworthy and elect lives, and practice and know all virtue? By so doing, the holy angels, we affirm, dwell in glory in heaven; for it is written, "Bless the Lord all you His hosts; His ministers who do His will" (Ps. 102:21).

For by adhering to the will of their Lord, and fulfilling that righteousness which transcends human things, they preserve their high estate, whereas those who acted otherwise fell therefrom.

But to gather to a head, and, so to speak, collect briefly the meaning of the words, we supplicate, that power may be given to the dwellers upon earth to do the will of God, and imitate the conduct practiced above in heaven by the holy angels. Let us see, therefore, as well as we can, in what way the powers above and the ranks of the holy angels successfully perform their duty. How do they honor God? Is it by sacrifices of blood? Is it by perfume and frankincense, as indeed the Israel after the flesh did? However, I think this is altogether incredible both to think and say. For it is rather true to affirm that they fulfill a spiritual and not a material service, ever crowning with lauds and praises the Creator of all, and fulfilling that righteousness which is suitable to holy spirits.

Those, therefore, who in their prayers ask that the will of God may be done also on earth, should "cleanse [them]selves from every defilement," leap out of the pitfalls of iniquity, and make "perfecting holiness in the fear of God" (2 Cor. 7:1), that as Paul also says, even while walking upon earth, their citizenship may be in heaven (cf. Phil. 3:20).

And above all others let those who belong to the Jewish multitude, but have been enriched with the righteousness that is in Christ by faith, know that it is altogether fitting for them if they would fulfill the word of God, to cease from the shadows of the law, and abandon the service that consists in semblances and types, and choose rather the service which is spiritual, and pure, and immaterial.

For as the Savior somewhere said, "God is Spirit, and those who worship Him must worship in Spirit and Truth" (Jn. 4:24).[4]

The Will of God is to Live a Noble Life

For that the legal manner of service is not what He requires, is a thing in no respect difficult to see from the prophetic and apostolic writings. For by the word of Jeremiah He says, "Why bring you unto Me the frankincense from Sheba and cinnamon from a far country? Your whole burnt-offering is not acceptable, and your sacrifices please Me not" (Jer. 6:20).

And by the voice of David, "I will not take bullocks from your house, nor the goats out of your flocks...Should I eat the flesh of bulls, or drink the blood of goats?" (Ps. 49:9, 13). And the blessed Paul also shows that the service that is by the law is powerless unto justification, thus saying, "No one is justified by the law in the sight of God is evident, for 'the just shall live by faith'" (Gal. 3:11).

Therefore, the will of God which we pray may be done upon earth, is not that we should conform to the law, and live according to the grossness of its letter, but that we should endeavor to live by the gospel. And this is affected by a faith correct and free from error, and by a holy life, possessed of the sweet savor of every virtue, and proved by the testimony of good and noble conduct in every thing that is excellent.

---

[4] This verse is a favorite of St. Cyril, an is the subject of what is believed to be his very first work, entitled, On Worship of God in Spirit and Truth.

The Error of the Jews: Haughtiness and Stubbornness

And to explain also in another way the sense of what is laid before us, we say, that those who utter unto God the petition "Thy will be done, as in heaven so on earth," pray that they may see the cessation of sin. For the law of Moses was given unto the Israelites to be their schoolmaster; but those who received it paid but slight heed to its commands. They were "lovers of pleasure rather than lovers of God" (2 Tim. 3:4), and turned aside to follow their own will: for they wandered after the doctrines and commandments of men.

For God also somewhere said concerning them, "This people draw near to Me with their mouth, and they honor Me with their lips, but their heart is far from Me; and in vain do they worship Me, teaching the commandments and doctrines of men" (Is. 29:13). And He also said of them by the word of Jeremiah, "Hear, O earth; behold, I will bring evils upon this people, even the fruit of their rebellions; for they have not heeded My words, and they have rejected My law" (Jer. 6:19). Such then was the state of the Jews.

The Error of the Gentiles: Self-Justification

But that other multitude, spread over the whole earth, was in error in manifold ways. For they "served the creature rather than the Creator" (Rom. 1:25). And, having humbled their mind to submission unto unclean spirits, they were led by them readily and without understanding, into every thing base, and every kind of wickedness was honored among them, and their "glory is in their shame" (Phil. 3:19), as Scripture says.

The Saints

The saints therefore supplicate, that both of these, as well Israel as the Gentiles, may be counted worthy of peace from on high, and be comforted in that they were in misery, and caught, so to speak, in the net of sin, without possibility of escape: that having received the righteousness which is in Christ by faith, they may become pure, and skillful in every good work. For this reason they pray, "Thy will be done, on earth as it is in heaven."

For as I said, the will of God over all is that the dwellers upon earth should live saintly, piously, blamelessly, being washed from all impurity, and diligent in imitating the spiritual beauty of the spirits above in heaven; so that the Church on earth, being, as it were, the visible likeness and image of "the general assembly and Church of the firstborn" (Heb. 12:23) that is above, may please Christ; by Whom, and with Whom, to God the Father be praise and dominion with the Holy Spirit, forever and ever, Amen.

VI
Homily 75:

Give Us this Day the Bread of Our Necessity (Luke 11:3)

Those who possess earthly riches invite to their house such of their friends as they wish to honor, and setting before them a costly banquet, make them enjoy themselves, though providing for them nothing further than the satiating of the appetite. But the Savior and Lord of all, feasts us not with bodily enjoyments; for this is profitless, and injurious even to the body itself. Rather He banquets with spiritual feasts the hearts of those who would live virtuously, bestowing on them the saving doctrine of the gospel, by means of which a man becomes full of all good, and an heir of eternal life. And what I have said is clearly taught us in the passage now set before us. For when you pray, He says, you must say, "Give us every day the bread of our necessity."

Praying for this Bread is Not Contrary to Pious Living

But some, perhaps, may think and even say, that it is unsuitable and not fitting for the saints to ask of God these corporeal things; and may therefore divert what is said to a spiritual sense; and affirm that they ask neither for earthly bread, nor that for the body, but for He Who came down from above, from heaven, and gave life to the world (Jn. 6:33).

And I too without all doubt would say, that it most becomes the saints earnestly to endeavor to be accounted worthy of spiritual gifts. We must, however, also understand, that though they ask simple bread, and this is what the Savior bids them do, that their address to God is nevertheless free from all blame, and suitable to the piety of their lives. For examine what is the sense concealed in these words, and with what doctrines it is pregnant. For in that

He commanded to ask for the bread, that is, for the food for a day. It is evident that He does not permit them to possess anything but requires them rather to practice a saint-like poverty. For to ask is not the part of those who have, but of those rather who are in need of what the body indispensably requires and cannot do without.

Even Those Who Possess Things Should ask for this Bread

Should then anyone who is in want of nothing, say unto the Omniscient God, "Give us the bread of a day," he would of course seem to wish to receive in derision, or perhaps even to ridicule the meaning of the command, and to imagine as some do, that "The Lord does not see, neither does the God of Jacob understand" (Ps. 93:7). By this very command therefore, inasmuch as they ask what they have not, we may perceive, that He does not wish His disciples to set their desire upon wealth. And this He is found elsewhere clearly enjoining: "Therefore do not worry, saying, 'What shall we eat?' or 'What shall we drink?' or 'What shall we wear?' For after all these things the Gentiles seek. For your heavenly Father knows that you need all these things. But seek first the kingdom of God and His righteousness, and all these things shall be added to you" (Mt. 6:31-33).

"Daily Bread" or "Bread of the Morrow"?

The word ἐπιούσιος[5] applied here to the bread, some explain as meaning that which is coming, and about to be

[5] The meaning of the word ἐπιούσιος, has greatly troubled interpreters. Perhaps the most common translation has been "daily bread" or the bread given day by day. However, St. Cyril offers two other explanations. The first dervies from ἔπειμι, to come upon, or from combining the participle

given in the future world, understanding it again spiritually: while others give the word a different sense. But if it is true, that the bread men mention when they pray, is that which is to be given them in the world to come, why do they add, "Give it us every day?" For by this we may see, that what they request is their daily provision, asking not as loving wealth, but as free from all earthly anxiety.

We must explain therefore ἐπιούσιος as meaning that which is necessary and sufficient. The blessed Paul has somewhere applied this phrase to Christ the Savior of us all, with a slight alteration; for he said that He has prepared "for Himself a people περιούσιος" (Tit. 2:14), using περιούσιος instead of ἐπιούσιος, and meaning a people sufficient, and not falling short of perfectness. When therefore they ask food for the day, understand, that they offer the request as men free from the desire of riches, and who count it their boast to be entirely destitute of earthly things.

ἐπιοῦσα with ἡμέρα, to signify tomorrow's bread. St. Jerome mentions this is the reading of the apocryphal Hebrew gospel. This reading suggests prayer for the next day's gifts as well as the bread of eternal life. Tertullian, St. Cyprian, and St. Augustine all relate this to a daily Eucharist which was offered in the West. St. Augustine also understands the daily bread as the Word of God and the blessings received from the altar (Sermon 56). St. Cyril's second derivation from ἐπὶ and οὐσία (which he supports by the analogy of περιούσιος, a word coined by the Septuagint), as ἐπιούσιος by the Evangelists. This gives the meaning of bread which exceeds our absolute needs, that is abundant, necessary or barely sufficient, or as St. Cyril renders it, αὐτάρκης. The Peshitta and Philoxenian translations both agree with this latter rendering of "our necessary bread." St. John Chrysostom further relates this to that bread necessary for one day, since one is not to "worry about tomorrow" (Homily XIX on Matthew 6:8). Others say daily bread is Christ Himself, the Eucharist, and the Manna from Heaven.

Living for Necessity and Fighting Against Desires

For it is fitting for those who are appointed to the priesthood, to be free from all worldly distraction and care, whoring after none of those things which overwhelm men with necessary cares, and cast them as in a recession into the filth of worldly lusts. "For the love of money is the root of all kinds of evil" (1 Tim. 6:10). And it is right that I should say to those who would renounce such faults, that they must strip off for the world what belongs to it, deny these bodily things, and seek from God those things only which are necessary for existence. [Thus, they will] protest against the weakness of the body, which constantly requires food; and ready, were it lawful utterly to escape from it, and life could so be prolonged, even to accept this with great joy.

For just as those who know how to contend in bodily strife, and are skilled in the combats of the games, strip off even their garments, and stand up manfully against the vigorous strength of their opponents; so also the saints, withdrawing from all worldly anxiety, and bodily lusts; and careless even of having abundance of food, and stripping as I said to oppose Satan and the enemies of the truth, apply themselves to the contests of the priestly office, and conquer as combatants.

And the divine Paul also somewhere said of those that war in the flesh, "No one engaged in warfare entangles himself with the affairs of this life, that he may please him who enlisted him as a soldier" (2 Tim. 2:4). For he goes forth to combat, not loaded with excesses, but on the contrary only taking with him such equipment as are fit for warriors.

Complete Consecration of the Saints

Therefore, it is fitting for the saints–as having a combat to wrestle "against flesh and blood, [and] against principalities, against powers, against the rulers of the darkness of this age, against spiritual hosts of wickedness in the heavenly places" (Eph. 6:12)–to be so well girt in mind, as not to be open to the grasp of those who resist them, and who war against the message which they proclaim.

And it is right also for them to be single-minded, that is, to think only of those things which please the Lord, not being partly given up unto worldly anxiety, but being all of them entirely holy and without blame, so to make their conduct a sacrifice unto God. For it is written, "And every sacrifice of a priest shall be thoroughly burned" (Lev. 6:23).

For the lives of the worldly are "divided"[6] according to the expression of the blessed Paul (1 Cor. 7:34). But this is not the case among the saints; for they are entirely consecrated, completely holy, emitting a sweet aroma to God. This, we say, is a whole burnt-offering. But when anything unsaintly is found in any, it pollutes the sacrifice, alters and divides it. Rather, filth is mingled with the ointment; for its sweet aroma has utterly perished.

Trust that God is Your Provider

But the love of money is an unsavory thing; and the being anxious for the things of the body; for God has

---

[6] St. Cyril evidently punctuates this verse in the same way as the Vulgate: "The married man is anxious about the things of the world to please his wife, and is divided."

everywhere promised the saints that they shall not want (Ps. 22:1). If then we do not believe that He will grant this, we become partakers of the unbelief of the Jews. For when God over all wonderfully and ineffably brought out for them water from the rock, they murmured at Him saying; "Why is God unable to prepare a table in the wilderness?" (Ps. 77:18).

And why can He not, and how should He not, give what He has promised? For all men of good character abide faithfully by their words. And how shall God Who transcends all, be false in anything that He has promised? Men moreover, after having promised some good, are often too weak to fulfill their engagements. But, since the Lord of Powers knows no weakness and does whatever He wishes without labor and with ease, how shall not He accomplish whatsoever He promised to men?

Therefore, "casting all [our] care upon Him" (1 Pet. 5:7), let us ask of Him what suffices for life–food, that is to say, and clothing, and whatever is sufficient for us–avoiding all wish to be rich, as that which threatens us with destruction. For if this is our will, Christ will accept and bless us; by Whom, and with Whom, to God the Father be praise and dominion with the Holy Spirit, forever and ever, Amen.

VII
Homily 76:

And Forgive Us our Sins: For we also Forgive Everyone who is Indebted to Us
(Luke 11:4)

The blessed prophet Isaiah, when revealing the way of salvation by the preaching of the Gospel, thus somewhere speaks, "There shall be there a pure way, and it shall be called the holy way" (Is. 35:8). For it leads those who walk thereon unto holiness by a spiritual service, and a righteousness superior to the law. We remember also Christ, Who says to those who love Him; "Truly I say unto you, that unless your righteousness exceeds that of the Scribes and Pharisees, you shall not enter the kingdom of God" (Mt. 5:20).

Imitate the Longsuffering and Forgiveness of God

And I say that it is the duty of those who have been called by faith to the acknowledgment of the glory of our universal Savior Christ, and have Him for their Head (Eph. 5:23, Col. 1:18), to delight in imitating His actions, and be in earnest in letting their light shine by holy conduct, such as was unknown to them of old time. "For all things have become new in Christ" (2 Cor. 5:17). He requires, therefore, His disciples to be gentle (2 Tim. 2:24) and slow to anger (Jam. 1:9), so that they may be able to say blamelessly in their prayers, "Forgive us our sins: for we also forgive everyone that is indebted unto us."

O, what great and admirable skill! What clever thought! Or rather, "Oh, the depth of the riches, both of the wisdom and knowledge of God!" (Rom. 11:33). He first commands them to ask forgiveness of the sins they commit; then to confess that they also entirely forgive others. [Only then], if I may so say, they [may] ask God to imitate the long suffering which they practice. And that same gentleness which they show to their fellow servants, they pray that they may receive in equal measure from God, Who gives justly, and knows how to show mercy to every man.

Come, therefore, and let us endeavor to perceive more clearly the meaning of the prayer, by entering upon a more extended and exact consideration of the passage before us. As I said, therefore, He has commanded us when we draw near to say, "Forgive us our sins."

God is Merciful to the Humble

And we will examine, if you please, what the benefit is which we receive from this. Those who speak this way, then, are not arrogant. They do not think great things of themselves; nor do they vaunt themselves over the weak, but, as Scripture says, "they know themselves" (Prov. 8:10). They are not like that ignorant and haughty Pharisee, who even made the Lord his witness, according to the parable which says: "Two men went up to the temple to pray, one a Pharisee and the other a tax collector. The Pharisee stood and prayed thus with himself, 'God, I thank You that I am not like other men–extortioners, unjust, adulterers, or even as this tax collector. I fast twice a week; I give tithes of all that I possess.' And the tax collector, standing afar off, would not so much as raise his eyes to heaven, but beat his breast, saying, 'God, be merciful to me a sinner!' I tell you, this man went down to his house justified rather than the other" (Lk. 18:10-14).

Observe, therefore, how ruinous it is to vaunt oneself over those who are weak, imagining that our conduct is in no respect whatsoever worthy of blame. We ought rather to consider and reflect, that "we all stumble in many things"

(Jam. 3:1) and, so to speak, are always in sins, sometimes, even involuntarily. For it is written, "Who can understand his transgressions?" (Ps. 18:13).

We find also the blessed Psalmist very anxious in making his supplications to God, and plainly saying, "Both cleanse me from my secret sins: and from the deeds of others spare Your servant, lest they overpower me: then shall I be blameless, and purified from great sin" (Ps. 18:13-14).

And further also, the very patient Job offered sacrifices for the unknown, or rather undiscovered sins of his sons, considering and saying, "It may be my sons have spoken evil in their heart against God" (Job 1:5). We remember also the very wise Paul, who, when he had written, "For I know of nothing against myself," thoughtfully added, "yet I am not justified by this; but He who judges me is the Lord" (1 Cor. 4:4).

It is therefore greatly to our profit constantly to fall down before God, Who loves what is good, and say, "Forgive us our sins." For He said by one of the holy prophets, "Declare first your unlawfulnesses, that you may be justified" (Is. 43:26). And inasmuch as this was known to the blessed David, he thus sings, "I said that I will confess of myself my iniquity to the Lord; and You forgave the wickedness of my heart" (Ps. 31:5).

God Rejects the Proud and Is Severe to the Stubborn

For God readily accepts, and has mercy on those who do not forget their offenses, but fall down before Him, and ask of Him forgiveness: but He is severe, and very justly so, upon the stubborn and the proud, and on him who in his great ignorance acquits himself of blame. For He said to one thus disposed, "Behold, I have a suit against you, because you say, I have not sinned" (Jer. 2:35).

For who can boast that he has a pure heart? Or who can have confidence that he is undefiled by sins? The road then to salvation, and which delivers those who earnestly walk thereon from the wrath of God, is the confession of offenses, and to say in our prayers to Him Who purifies the wicked, "Forgive us our sins."

Remember the Judgment of God

There is also another way in which it benefits us. For those verily who own that they have sinned, and wish to obtain pardon from God, necessarily fear Him, as One Who is about to be the Judge, they are not forgetful of God's awesome judgment seat. For, as the very wise Paul writes: "For we must all appear before the judgment seat of Christ, that each one may receive the things done in the body, according to what he has done, whether good or bad" (2 Cor. 5:10).

Those in whose mind the conviction is present must stand before Him, and make their defense. And if they are accused of wicked conduct, they will suffer bitter punishment. But, they will be praised if they have well and wisely led the life that is in the flesh on earth. Thirst, on the one hand, for the forgiveness of the sins they have already committed, that they may escape the unending torment and eternal punishment; and, on the other, they hasten to live uprightly and blamelessly, that they may receive the crown that becomes the excellence of their lives (1 Pet. 5:4). For so will the Judge be gentle towards them and not remember evil. "For the iniquity," He says, "of the wicked shall not harm him in the day that he shall repent of his iniquity" (Ez. 33:12).

Do not let anyone imagine that it is lawful for men without distinction to say, "Forgive us our iniquities." For it is not fitting for those who still continue in wickedness, and wish to do so to the last, to say, "Forgive us our sins," but for those, rather, who have abandoned their former wicked deeds, and now earnestly desire to live fitting of saints. Were it not so, nothing would prevent men who are still wicked–smiters of their fathers, and matricides, and adulterers, and sorcerers, and whoever are guilty of these most abominable crimes–to continue in practice of them, cherish their evil propensities unchanged, be polluted by the pursuit of every thing that is base; and nevertheless to draw near, and presumptuously say, "Forgive us our sins."

Be Slow to Anger and Quick to Forgive

For with good reason the Savior of all and Lord did not conclude this clause of the prayer at this point, but commanded us to add, "For we also ourselves have forgiven every one who is indebted to us." But this is fitting only for those to say, who have chosen a virtuous life, and are practicing without remissness that will of God, which, as Scripture says, is "good and acceptable and perfect" (Rom. 12:2). These honor a long-suffering temper, and acquit of all blame those who have wronged them. And even if anyone afflicts them, they think nothing of the matter. To be slow to anger, then, is a virtue altogether excellent, and the fruit of that love which the wise Paul even declares to be "the fulfillment of the law" (Rom. 13:10).

The Malady of Anger

And consider, I pray, the exceeding beauty of this virtue, even from the deformity of the vice opposed to it. For anger is in truth a serious malady. Whoever is subject to it in mind becomes irritable and ill-tempered, harsh and stubborn, the abode and habitation of wrath and vexation.

[And when such anger is] extended for a while continuously, it cannot be charmed away. He constantly beholds with evil eyes whoever has wronged him. He watches him sternly and seeks for time and place in which to injure him, and generally not in equal measure, but many times greater than the wrong. He is concealed and plotting. Is not such a one full of all deformity, hateful to God, rejected by Him, and therefore in utter misery?

"For the ways of the angry," as it is written, "are to death" (Prov. 12:28). But he who is simple, and not angry, is full of forbearance–not so much the forbearance which men practice, but that which comes from above, and from God. His heart is not subject to the fester of vexation: it masters its anger, and repels the bitter feelings which spring therefrom. He is forgiving, kind to his companions, gentle and friendly, and humbles himself to the infirmity of his neighbor.

The Long-Suffering of Christ and the Disciples

Such was the character of the disciples of the Savior: for the blessed Paul wrote: "Being reviled, we bless; being persecuted, we endure; being defamed, we entreat" (1 Cor. 4:12-13). For they have grown like their Lord, "Who, when He was reviled, did not revile in return; when He suffered, He did not threaten, but committed Himself to Him Who judges righteously" (1 Pet. 2:23).

We must ask, therefore, from God the forgiveness of the sins we have committed, when we have ourselves first forgiven whoever have offended in ought, provided that their sin is against us, and not against the glory of the supreme God. For over such actions we are not lords, but only over those which have been committed against ourselves. And by thus forgiving the brethren what they do to us, we shall then certainly find Christ, the Savior of all, gentle and ready to show us mercy: by Whom and with Whom to God the Father be praise and dominion, with the Holy Spirit, forever and ever, Amen.

VIII
Homily 77:

And Lead Us not into Temptation but Deliver Us from the Evil One
(Luke 11:4)

O all you who love the divine will and are enamored with a blameless life, draw near unto God over all, and say, "Show me Your ways, O Lord, and teach me Your paths" (Ps. 24:4). For all wisdom and understanding is from Him; and the knowledge of all good comes to us from above from the supreme throne, as from a fountain; and no man can accomplish any thing praiseworthy, unless he receive the ability from Him. This, He teaches us Himself, saying, "Without Me you can do nothing" (Jn. 15:5). Therefore, He gives to every man all things whatever wherein they can justly glory, now leads us on to another of those things which are necessary to salvation. For He commands us when we are instant in prayer to say, "Lead us not into temptation."

"But Deliver us from Evil" (Mt. 5:13)

With these words Luke concludes the prayer; but Matthew is found to add, "but deliver us from evil" (Mt. 5:13). And there is a certain close connection in the clauses: for plainly it follows from men not being led into temptation, that they are also delivered from evil; or perhaps, were anyone to say, that the not being led into it is the same as the being delivered from it, he would not err from the truth.

But let us consider this: Does the Savior and Lord of all wish His friends to be cowardly? Are they to be lazy and abject, and in earnest rather in avoiding the contest than in winning renown?

And yet the Spirit said in the book of Psalms, "Be of good courage, and let your heart be strengthened, all you who hope in the Lord" (Ps. 30:25). And the Savior Himself somewhere says, "Blessed are those who are persecuted for righteousness' sake: for theirs is the kingdom of heaven" (Mt. 5:10).

If then He crowns with such splendid honors him who is persecuted–and to be persecuted is undeniably a temptation–in what sense does He command them to avoid temptation?

Toil Against Tribulations

For certainly it is not inactivity, an unprofitable delay, or a thankless sloth which render those trained for gymnastic contests successful, worthy of honors, and the clapping of hands; but, on the contrary, severe toil. Moreover, it is not in time of peace that one sees the man who is well acquainted with the tactics of war, bold and tried in battle, but he must have shown himself a hardy combatant against the enemy.

And why then does Christ, so to speak, even hamstring those who love Him, by making them say, "Lead us not into temptation?"

To this we reply, gathering after our manner those ideas which are best, that He does not wish His followers to be abject, nor yet lazy in any other way; that He even incites them to courageousness in all things praiseworthy, saying, "Enter by the narrow gate...Because narrow is the gate and difficult is the way which leads to life, and there are few who find it" (Mt. 7:13,14).

There must, therefore, be in us an unchangeable and strong spirit of enthusiasm: and a mind patient in endurance, such as was that of the blessed Paul, who said, "Who will separate us from the love of Christ? Shall hardship, or distress, or persecution, or famine, or nakedness, or peril, or sword?" (Rom. 8:35).

Think Humbly of the Battle; Do not be Overconfident

But even though we be thus minded, and attain to these measures of strength, yet we must think humbly of ourselves, being "poor in spirit" (Mt. 5:3), according to the Savior's word, and not imagine that always and necessarily we shall conquer all temptations.

For sometimes an unendurable alarm falling upon the mind of a man terrifies it into abject fear; as also does Satan, who hates whatever is good; and the severity of the temptation unbends sometimes even the most courageous mind. So do the violent and unendurable blows of the waves dash to pieces a firmly built and well-manned ship: and so does a dense mass of darts shot from the flames of the enemy put to flight the most steadfast soldier.

No one, therefore, should be overconfident or rash in encountering temptations, even though he is brave in mind. But rather, let us reflect upon the infirmity of our mind, and fear with soberness, lest perhaps we prove a cause of ridicule to our tempters, by not being able to bear the brunt of the battle.

Let us, therefore, pray that we may not be tempted; for it is a thing difficult to escape from, and difficult to most men to endure unto the end. But when the state of affairs summons us of necessity thereto, then indeed, exerting all our strength, we must enter the conflict, and struggle for our souls, nothing fearing, but, on the contrary, calling to mind what Christ the Savior of all said to us; "Do not fear those who kill the body but cannot kill the soul. But rather fear Him Who is able to destroy both soul and body in hell" (Mt. 10:28). As also that holy apostle who thus wrote, "Blessed is the man who endures temptation; for when he has been approved, he will receive the crown of life which the Lord has promised to those who love Him" (Jam. 1:12).

The Temptation of Heresy

There are however many kinds of temptation, of which two are of universal occurrence, common and very general. And what these are it behooves us to tell. There are in the world many heresies, false apostles, and false teachers, who gathering the wearisomeness of frigid inventions and glorying in the arts of worldly wisdom, adulterate the language of the sacred proclamations and multiply blasphemous words against their own heads. As the Psalmist says, "lift up their horn on high, speaking iniquity against God" (Ps. 75:5). Yes, [they act] against God the Logos, the Maker of all, they say [He] is to be reckoned among those things that were made by Him; [and that He] is a servant, not a Son; a creature, and not the Lord.

These resisting the champions of the truth persecute those whose choice it is to hold sound doctrine, and who defend the divine glory, and endeavor to crown the Only-Begotten Logos of God with incomparable praises. When, therefore, any temptation arrives on this account, do not be found one who throws away his shield, nor a soldier who runs from the battle, nor an athlete destitute alike of skill and courage. Do not wish an unseasonable peace, the cause of future ruin; but remember that Christ the Savior of all said, "Do not think that I came to bring peace on earth. I did not come to bring peace but a sword" (Mt. 10:34).

And if perhaps it happens that the persecutors possess worldly power, do not fear the harm they can do you, nor the danger even of blood, and the risk of life. But, remember again the exhortation of the holy apostle, who says, "Therefore, let those who suffer according to the will of God commit their souls to Him in doing good, as to a faithful Creator"(1 Pet. 4:19). And again, "But let none of you suffer as a murderer, a thief, an evildoer, or as a busybody in other people's matters. Yet if anyone suffers as a Christian, let him not be ashamed, but let him glorify God in this matter" (1 Pet. 4:15-16).

For it follows as a matter of course upon having to suffer, that we shall justly be accounted worthy of eternal honors. The struggle is not unrewarded; the labor is not in vain. For, as Paul said, "God is not unjust to forget your work and labor of love which you have shown toward His Name" (Heb. 6:10).

These, then, are the conflicts ordained for all who fear God, to give the proof of him who knows how to endure patiently. For the blessed martyrs are crowned, as having fought the good fight, finished the race, and kept the faith (cf. 2 Tim. 4:7).

Conquering the Temptations of the Passions

Furthermore, other kinds of temptations there are besides this, common, so to speak, to every one, but which happen to each one differently. For as one of the holy apostles said, "Let no one say when he is tempted, 'I am tempted by God'; for God cannot be tempted by evil, nor does He Himself tempt anyone. But each one is tempted when he is drawn away by his own desires and enticed. Then, when desire has conceived, it gives birth to sin; and sin, when it is full- grown, brings forth death" (Jam. 1:13-15).

A struggle therefore and great danger is laid upon every one, lest he fall into sin, and be led away from that which is seemly, wandering into wrongful deeds. Violent is the force of passions, and there wars against the mind of every one a diverse crowd and furious multitude of base pleasures. For some humble men [fall] into fleshly lust and filthy lewdnesses; while others lead them to the desire of gain, making their victims lovers of debased treasures, and drawing them on to every blameful crime.

Well, therefore, does it become us who are exposed to such serious evils, even though yet we have not fallen into them, to pray, saying, "Lead us not into temptation, but deliver us from evil." For it is good for a man to run his course apart from evil. But if temptation attacks, then be brave and unconquerable; rebuke the flesh; put a bridle on the mind; ask aid of God, the safety granted by power from on high. Be established and confirmed, not feeble, not easy to be ensnared. Rather, be cautious, and a lover of God more than a lover of pleasure. For then, He will aid you and grant you victory Who is Savior and Lord of all: by Whom and with Whom, to God the Father be praise and dominion, with the Holy Spirit, forever and ever, Amen.

Ⲇⲟⲝⲁⲥⲓ ⲟ̀ⲑⲉⲟⲥ ⲏ̀ⲙⲱⲛ

St. Cyril of Alexandria

(ca. 380-444 AD)

Also known as the Pillar of Faith, this father is the twenty-fourth Patriarch of the See of St. Mark. St. Cyril was the son of the sister of Pope Theophilus (23rd patriarch), who trained him in Theology and Philosophy at the School of Alexandria, then sent him to the monastery of St. Macarius in the wilderness. There he studied the Church books and sayings of the fathers for five years under a righteous monk named Sarapamon. Later he was sent to the honorable bishop Abba Serapion, and he increased in wisdom and knowledge. After St. Cyril returned to Alexandria, Pope Theophilus ordained him a deacon, appointed him a preacher in the cathedral, and made St. Cyril his scribe. When his uncle departed in 412, St. Cyril was enthroned as 24th patriarch of Alexandria on 20 Babeh, 128 AM (October 17, 412). He is famous for his exceptional biblical exegesis and Christological formulas, which he used to defend the faith while presiding over the Council of Ephesus against Nestorius. He remained a pope for 31 years. He is one of the greatest fathers of the ancient Church, whose life and teachings have been decisive in shaping the Orthodox tradition. We commemorate his departure on 3 Abib.

Printed in Great Britain
by Amazon

40930967R00041